SUPERSTARS
of
PRO
FOOTBALL

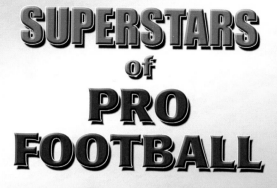

Rudolph T. Heits

Mason Crest Publishers
Philadelphia

MASON CREST PUBLISHERS, INC.
370 Reed Road
Broomall PA 19008
(866) MCP-BOOK (toll free)
www.masoncrest.com

Printed in the United States of America.

CPISA compliance information: Batch#060110-FB4. For further information, contact
Mason Crest Publishers at 610-543-6200.

First printing

9 8 7 6 5 4 3 2 1

Library of Congress Cataloging-in-Publication Data

Heits, Rudolph T.
  Ben Roethlisberger / Rudolph T. Heits.
      p. cm. — (Superstars of pro football)
  Includes bibliographical references and index.
ISBN 978-1-4222-1664-4 (hc)
ISBN 978-1-4222-1984-3 (pb)
  1. Roethlisberger, Ben, 1982-   —Juvenile literature. 2. Football players—United
States—Biography—Juvenile literature. I. Title.
GV939.R64H45 2010
796.332092—dc22
[B]
                                                                    2010008617

◀◀ CROSS-CURRENTS ▶▶

In the ebb and flow of the currents of life we are each influenced
by many people, places, and events that we directly experience or
have learned about. Throughout the chapters of this book you will
come across CROSS-CURRENTS reference bubbles. These bubbles
direct you to a CROSS-CURRENTS section in the back of the
book that contains fascinating and informative
articles and related pictures. Go on. ▶▶

◀◀ CONTENTS ▶▶

BIG BEN SAVES THE DAY

Most football fans expected one of the quarterbacks to come out firing in the American Football Conference (AFC) divisional playoff game of January 15, 2006. They just assumed it would be Peyton Manning of the Indianapolis Colts rather than Ben Roethlisberger of the Pittsburgh Steelers.

Indianapolis was, after all, a famously pass-oriented team, and Manning was one of the slickest quarterbacks in the entire National Football League (NFL). A keen student of the game in his eighth year as a pro, he had the experience and the ability to quickly size up an opposing defense and locate an open receiver. He also had the arm to deliver strong, accurate passes. Manning held the NFL single-season records for touchdown passes and for **passer**

Ben Roethlisberger has become one of the National Football League's most popular and successful quarterbacks. In his first six years in the league, Ben's teams have won almost 70 percent of their games, including two Super Bowl titles.

rating (a statistic that measures a quarterback's efficiency). During the 2005 regular season, with Manning as the field general and a corps of talented receivers led by Marvin Harrison and Reggie Wayne, Indianapolis had ripped through opposing defenses, putting up more points than all but one of the NFL's 32 teams.

Somewhat lost in the offensive fireworks, however, was the fact that the Colts also fielded a fine defense. They had, in fact, surrendered fewer points than all but one NFL team.

Not surprisingly, this combination of explosive offense and stingy defense allowed Indianapolis to outscore opponents by an average of 12 points per game, the biggest margin in the NFL. Indy also compiled the league's best record, winning 14 games and losing just 2. Heading into the postseason, the Colts were favorites to win the Super Bowl.

Grinding out Victories

In contrast to the flashy, offensive-minded Colts, the 2005 Pittsburgh Steelers favored a more grinding style of play. Their tough, bruising defense limited opponents' trips to the end zone. In points allowed, Pittsburgh was tied for third in the NFL, right behind Indianapolis. On offense, the Steelers looked to rush the ball frequently—using their potent running-back **tandem** of speedy Willie Parker and massive Jerome "the Bus" Bettis—and to pass sparingly.

CROSS-CURRENTS

The Pittsburgh Steelers have been one of the NFL's most successful franchises. For a brief history of the team, see page 46.

Pittsburgh head coach Bill Cowher liked the conservative offensive scheme in part because it didn't require his young quarterback, Ben Roethlisberger, to do too much. Quarterback is football's most difficult position to master. It is quite common for QBs—even those who have had storied college careers—to struggle mightily in their first few pro seasons. Many never live up to their promise. The pressure on an NFL quarterback, particularly a young one, is intense.

Under Pittsburgh's 2005 offensive scheme, however, Ben Roethlisberger didn't have to be spectacular for the team to succeed. But he did have to be consistent. Above all, Cowher expected his 23-year-old, second-year QB to avoid costly mistakes. Stout defense and a pounding running game, the coach believed, could carry the team.

Pittsburgh head coach Bill Cowher gives instructions to his young quarterback during a timeout in the January 2006 playoff game against the Colts. During the season, Cowher had kept the Steelers' offense simple to keep pressure off Ben. But in the playoffs, the coach allowed Ben to open things up with passes down the field.

The formula had worked pretty well throughout the 2005 regular season. Big Ben—who at 6'5" tall and 241 pounds lived up to his nickname—finished with a respectable 17 touchdown passes, against just nine interceptions and one lost fumble. More important, Pittsburgh won 9 of the 12 games Ben started (injuries sidelined him for the remaining 4 games).

Playoff Surprise

During the five-game winning streak that Pittsburgh took into its January 15 divisional playoff matchup with Indianapolis, Ben Roethlisberger had averaged just 178 passing yards per game, and he'd thrown for only six touchdowns total. But he'd also thrown only two interceptions. The Colts had little reason to suspect that Bill Cowher would deviate from his successful script by having his quarterback take to the air early. But that is exactly what happened.

Following the opening kickoff, the Steelers' offense took the field at their own 20-yard line. As the 58,000 Colts fans packing Indianapolis's RCA Dome let loose a deafening roar, Big Ben dropped back to pass on the first play from scrimmage. He failed to connect with his intended target, wide receiver Antwaan Randle El. Ben again threw on second down, this time completing a 36-yard strike to tight end Heath Miller. That took the Steelers past midfield and into Colts territory. Eight plays and about five minutes later, Big Ben capped the drive with a six-yard touchdown toss to Randle El. The Indianapolis defense seemed to be back on its heels. Seven of the drive's 10 plays from scrimmage had been passes.

Later in the first quarter, Ben led the Steelers on another scoring drive. This one, which covered 72 yards, took less than three minutes. The big play was a 45-yard bomb to wide receiver Hines Ward. Two plays later, Big Ben rolled to his right and zipped a ball just beyond the reach of Colts defensive back Mike Doss. Heath Miller caught the perfectly thrown pass for a seven-yard touchdown. Pittsburgh led by a score of 14–0.

Pittsburgh's defense, meanwhile, was shutting down Peyton Manning and the high-flying Colts offense. Indianapolis didn't even get a first down until nearly 13 minutes were gone in the first quarter. The Colts' single sustained drive of the first half netted only three points, on a Mike Vanderjagt field goal with 1:23 left in the second quarter. To the dismay of the hometown crowd, the teams went into their locker rooms at halftime with Pittsburgh holding a 14–3 lead.

"The Tackle"

Indy's frustrations resumed after the intermission as the Pittsburgh defense continued to hold firm. On offense the Steelers throttled back on the surprising aerial attack of the first half. Increasingly, they put the ball into the hands of Willie Parker and Jerome Bettis. The running backs pounded ahead for first downs, in the process consuming big chunks of time on the game clock. The only scoring of the third quarter came on a Pittsburgh drive that featured a run by Parker followed by five straight runs by Bettis. The Bus smashed through the Colts' line from one yard out, putting the Steelers up by a score of 21–3 with under 1:30 left in the third quarter.

Pittsburgh seemed to be in command. But, as team after team had discovered throughout the 2005 season, corralling the Colts' offense for an entire game was nearly impossible. Less than one minute into the fourth quarter, Manning connected with tight end Dallas Clark for a 50-yard touchdown. Pittsburgh's lead had been cut to 21–10.

Later in the quarter, Manning marched his team 80 yards for another TD. After a successful two-point conversion, the Colts trailed by just a field goal, 21–18, with 4:24 left on the game clock.

Pittsburgh took no chances on the ensuing **possession**. The Steelers ran three plays from scrimmage and punted.

The Colts got the ball back at their own 18-yard line, with 2:31 remaining on the clock. This time, however, the Steelers' defense was unyielding. On first down, Manning completed a pass to Edgerrin James for a paltry two-yard gain. The Colts' QB fell victim to a **sack** on second down, losing eight yards in the process. An incomplete pass on third down left Indianapolis staring at fourth-and-16. Pittsburgh brought the **blitz**, and Steelers linebackers Joey Porter and James Farrior collaborated on another sack, dropping Manning at the two-yard line.

On the Pittsburgh sideline, head coach Bill Cowher took off his headset and erupted into a double-fist-pump celebration. The Steelers had punched their ticket to the AFC championship game. Or so everyone thought.

Though the game clock showed just 1:20, Indianapolis had

Indianapolis defenders Dwight Freeney (#93) and Raheem Brock (#79) can't stop Ben from completing a pass. Ben's two first-quarter touchdown passes gave Pittsburgh a 14–0 lead.

all three of its timeouts remaining. If the Steelers snapped the ball and had Ben Roethlisberger kneel down four times, the Colts could get the ball back—albeit pinned deep in their own territory—with perhaps 20 or 25 seconds left and trailing by a field goal. So Cowher decided to run a play in an attempt to put the game completely out of reach. He inserted his goal-line offense—a lineup of big blockers—and called for a Jerome Bettis rush. It seemed like a safe bet: the sure-handed Bettis hadn't fumbled once the entire season. But when the Bus took the handoff and rumbled toward the goal line, Colts linebacker Gary Brackett delivered a hit that sent the football flying backward. The ball tumbled to the turf around the five-yard line.

Many quarterbacks confronting the situation would have panicked and immediately scrambled after the ball. But Ben Roethlisberger has always been an exceptionally calm person who never seems to lose his poise, not even in the midst of chaos on the **gridiron**. He recognized instantly that he was too far away to recover the fumble. And, with the Steelers' goal-line offense on the field, Big Ben knew that none of his teammates would be fast enough to chase down a Colt who recovered the ball if he moved forward and missed the initial tackle.

Indianapolis cornerback Nick Harper scooped up the football and made a beeline for the end zone, more than 90 yards away. Ben retreated, trying to slow Harper down while staying away from Colts blockers. Harper zigged and zagged. But he couldn't shake the Steelers' QB, who turned with him as the distance between the two players closed.

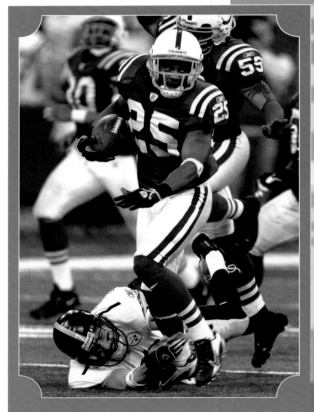

Heads-up play: Ben tackles the Colts' Nick Harper (#25), who had recovered a fourth-quarter fumble by Pittsburgh running back Jerome Bettis. The tackle prevented a touchdown and preserved the Steelers' 21–18 playoff victory over Indianapolis.

Finally, at the Colts' 35-yard line, Ben planted his feet and squared up to the cornerback. Harper juked and cut left. Ben lunged, catching enough of the cornerback's right ankle to trip him. Harper fell at the 42-yard line.

Ben's cool, smart response to Bettis's fumble and the ensuing runback had put him in a position to make the game-saving play Steelers fans would refer to fondly as "the Tackle." Pittsburgh's victory was sealed when Colts' kicker Mike Vanderjagt missed a 46-yard field goal with 21 seconds left.

After the game, the quiet, humble Ben downplayed his extraordinary effort. He said he was "very lucky" to bring Harper down, noting:

"It's one of those things where once in a blue moon Jerome fumbles and once in a blue moon I'm going to make that tackle."

Hines Ward wasn't shy about giving credit for the victory. The wide receiver spoke for all his teammates when he said:

"Ben saved the year for us with the tackle."

It would not be the last time that the young quarterback came through in a big way for his team.

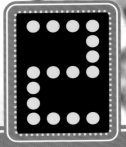

SMALL-TOWN HERO

Ben Roethlisberger took to sports from an early age, which is perhaps not surprising given his athletic pedigree. His mother, Ida, had been on her high school's softball, basketball, and track teams. His father, Ken, was a standout in football and baseball. He received a full scholarship to play quarterback at Georgia Tech University but saw his career cut short by a knee injury.

The only child of Ken and Ida Roethlisberger, Ben was born on March 2, 1982, in Lima, Ohio. Located in the northwestern part of the state, Lima is a small city, with a population of less than 50,000.

Ben (center, holding #1 jersey) poses with family members and friends after being selected by the Pittsburgh Steelers on NFL draft day in April 2004. Standing on the left are his father, Ken, and stepmother, Brenda. Carlee, Ben's younger sister, is standing to the right of him.

Ben was only two when his parents split up. After the divorce, he went to live with his father, who remarried. Ben became close to his stepmother, Brenda. But he also remained very close to his mom, with whom he spent every other weekend.

Ida Roethlisberger was on her way to pick Ben up at his father's house one Friday evening in 1990 when her car was hit by a truck. She died a short while later in the hospital. Today, Ben—who was eight years old at the time of the tragedy—is reluctant to talk about his mother. But he has a Chinese symbol for "mother" tattooed over his heart, and after every touchdown pass he throws, he points skyward to honor Ida's memory.

Findlay's Finest

In 1992, when Ben was 10, his family—which by now included a younger sister, Carlee—moved to Findlay, Ohio. The small, **blue-collar** town is about 45 miles south of Toledo. In Findlay, Ken Roethlisberger, an engineer by training, became the manager of a plant that manufactured automobile parts. His son, meanwhile, became a local sports legend.

Ben played youth football, basketball, and baseball. He excelled at all three but was especially fond of basketball.

At Findlay High School, Ben became the varsity basketball team's starting point guard in 1997, as a sophomore. His coach, Jerry Snodgrass, noticed how Ben already possessed extraordinary poise, awareness, and leadership skills, in addition to a knack for anticipating the flow of play—all of which would later serve him well in the NFL. Snodgrass told a reporter in 2005:

> **"Even when he was 15, Ben had a quiet command about him. One of the reasons Ben seems so calm is that he's always been a step ahead of everyone, always looking for an edge. . . ."**

Ben was picked as captain of the basketball team, and he became Findlay High's all-time leading scorer. He planned to play basketball in college.

But he also starred on, and was a captain of, Findlay's varsity baseball team. Ben played shortstop and was a .300 hitter.

Ben's high school football career, surprisingly, took a while to get off the ground. In his freshman season, he played quarterback on the junior varsity squad. The following year, he rode the bench on the varsity team as a backup quarterback. By his junior year, Ben believed he should be Findlay's starting QB. But the job went to the son of head coach Cliff Hite, who made Ben a wide receiver. Years later, Hite would tell a reporter that while he knew Ben wasn't happy with the arrangement, the young man never complained.

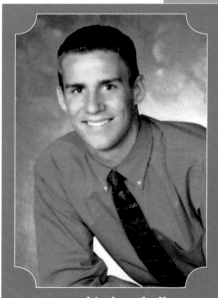

Ben starred in baseball, basketball, and football at Findlay High School in Ohio. This photo of Ben was taken during the 1999–2000 school year, when Ben was a senior.

Ben proved to be pretty good at catching the ball. As a junior wide receiver, he pulled down 57 receptions, including seven touchdowns, and Findlay won its conference championship. Still, the multitalented athlete, who was surprisingly quick and agile for his size—he stood 6'4" tall and weighed over 200 pounds—failed to attract the attention of college football coaches.

After his junior year of high school, Ben attended a summer camp at Miami University in Oxford, Ohio. He was throwing a football around with some buddies when an assistant coach of Miami's football team noticed him. As he watched, the coach became more and more amazed. Ben's throwing motion was smooth and flawless, and he had a rifle for an arm. Again and again, the football zipped out of Ben's hand and flew in a tight spiral right to its target. Surely this kid must be a top **recruit**. How was it possible, the coach wondered, that he didn't know who Ben was?

The explanation became clear when the coach talked to Ben and found out that Ben hadn't played quarterback on his high school team. Excited, the man rushed off to tell his boss, Miami head coach Terry Hoeppner, about the big kid with a big arm who had slipped under everybody's radar. Hoeppner decided to recruit Ben before coaches at other colleges found out just how much talent the young man had. It proved to be a wise decision.

With his son having graduated, Findlay High football coach Cliff Hite made Ben Roethlisberger his starting quarterback for the 1999 season. In his first game as QB, Ben threw six touchdown passes. The following day, Terry Hoeppner offered him a full scholarship to play football for the Miami University RedHawks.

Ben proved simply unstoppable as Findlay's quarterback. As he turned in one dominant performance after another, coaches from big-time college football programs began calling. They included John Cooper of Ohio State. The Buckeyes might have seemed like a good fit for Ben. They belonged to a major conference, the Big Ten, and were a perennial football powerhouse. If he played for Ohio State, Ben would have a national stage on which to showcase his talent.

But Ben liked Coach Hoeppner, and he appreciated the fact that Hoeppner had been interested in him before anyone else. Ben also

During his three seasons at Miami University of Ohio, Ben broke most of the school's passing records. The RedHawks won 27 of the 38 games (71 percent) that Ben started at quarterback, including the last 13 in a row.

suspected that, at a huge football school like Ohio State, he might be treated as a cog in a machine rather than an individual.

In the end, Ben spurned the scholarship offers from big-time football schools and signed on to play at Miami University. Miami of Ohio competed in a lesser-known athletic conference, the Mid-American Conference (MAC), but Ben would have the opportunity to be a four-year starter for the RedHawks.

Big Ben on Campus

Ben entered Miami University during the fall semester of 2000. His major was physical education.

During his first year at Miami, Ben was a **redshirt**. Under the rules of the National Collegiate Athletic Association (NCAA), college athletes are permitted only four seasons of competition in any sport. Redshirting allows an athlete to work out and practice with his team (but not play in any games) for one academic year while still retaining four seasons of eligibility for competition.

In 2001, Ben was installed as the starting quarterback for the RedHawks. He wore #7, the uniform number of longtime Denver Broncos QB John Elway. Elway had been Ben's childhood idol as well as the favorite player of Ben's mother, Ida.

Big Ben made a big splash in his first season as a college quarterback. He led the RedHawks to an exhilarating, come-from-behind victory over Akron with a 70-yard touchdown pass as time expired. In that game, played on October 13, Ben threw for 399 yards, setting a Miami University single-game passing record. The new record wouldn't last long, however. On November 17, in a game against Hawaii, Ben racked up 452 passing yards. His 40 completions and 53 attempted passes were also school records. By the end of the 2001 season, Ben had set RedHawk single-season records for passing yards (3,105), completions (241), touchdown passes (25), and completion percentage (.663). He was named the MAC Freshman of the Year, and he won Freshman All-America honors from the Football Writers Association of America.

In 2002, Ben proved that his freshman success had been no fluke. During his sophomore campaign, he broke his own Miami University single-season records by completing 271 passes and throwing for 3,238 yards. He also set a new single-game mark for completions (41), and he shattered the record for passing yards in a game, throwing for an astounding 525 yards against Northern Illinois on October 12.

Despite his gridiron heroics, Ben remained humble and down-to-earth, teammates and coaches at Miami would recall. When the team did well, he was quick to give credit to others. When the RedHawks lost, he invariably took responsibility himself.

Ben's remarkably calm demeanor also impressed those around him. Nothing ever seemed to rattle him, on the field or off. Ben's placid nature became something of a RedHawks team joke, and wide receiver Mike Larkin—who was the quarterback's roommate—decided to see whether he could make Ben lose his cool. Larkin swiped Ben's food out of the refrigerator. He turned off the TV while Ben—a huge video-game fan—was in the middle of a game. He sat behind Ben on the team bus and swatted at Ben's ears. Larkin recalled:

> **"I broke every roommate rule known to man to try and get to him, but nothing worked. ...Ben just has this weird calm to him no matter what's going on around him. I was the one who ended up snapping."**

Record Breaker

The 2003 season, Ben's junior year, didn't start out well for the Miami football team. In their first game, the RedHawks failed to score a touchdown and fell, 21–3, to Iowa. That would be the last time all season any team held Miami's offense, and Ben Roethlisberger, in check.

Following the loss to Iowa, Miami reeled off a dozen straight regular-season

Ben celebrates after receiving the GMAC Bowl Most Valuable Player Award, December 2003. The star quarterback threw four touchdown passes, leading Miami of Ohio to a 49–28 victory over Louisville in the bowl game.

victories. During this streak, the team averaged 45.8 points per game as Ben lit up defense after defense. He finished the regular season with 33 touchdown passes and 4,110 passing yards.

Miami, sporting a 12–1 record and ranked 15th nationally, earned an invitation to the 2003 GMAC Bowl. It was the school's first bowl appearance since 1986, and Ben ensured that the RedHawks made the most of the opportunity. On December 18, he scorched the Louisville Cardinals' defense, completing 21 of 33 passes for 376 yards, with four touchdowns and no interceptions. Miami won, 49–28, and Ben was named the GMAC Bowl's MVP.

Ben had established RedHawks single-season records for touchdown passes (37), passing yards (4,486), and completion percentage (69.1). Though he still had a season of eligibility left, he owned a host of RedHawks career records, including pass attempts (1,304), completions (854), and touchdown passes (80).

With an outstanding senior season, Ben had a chance to post some truly astronomical career numbers—and perhaps even contend for the **Heisman Trophy**. But he decided to forgo the opportunity to burnish his collegiate football credentials. After the GMAC Bowl, Ben announced that he would be skipping his senior season in order to enter the 2004 NFL draft.

CROSS-CURRENTS

The NFL's annual draft is the method by which teams select new players from the ranks of college football. For more information on the draft, turn to page 48.

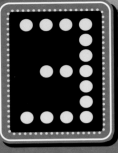

THE ROAD TO SUPER BOWL XL

The 2004 NFL draft, held April 24–25 at Madison Square Garden in New York City, began with the San Diego Chargers selecting University of Mississippi quarterback Eli Manning with the first pick. The Pittsburgh Steelers chose Ben Roethlisberger with the 11th pick in the first round.

Ben accepted a six-year contract that paid him a first-year base salary of $230,000, plus a $9 million signing bonus. Overnight, the 22-year-old was rich. But he seemed to have no pretensions. And Pittsburgh—with its blue-collar history and its small-city feel—appeared to be Ben Roethlisberger's kind of town. "From what I can tell," Ben told a reporter, "Pittsburgh is almost like a bigger version of Findlay."

In the early summer, Ben bought a townhouse in the Washington's Landing section of the Steel City. Neighbors

CROSS-CURRENTS

Controversy swirled around the 2004 NFL draft, and Eli Manning was at the center of it. Turn to page 49 for details.

described him as quiet, considerate, and down-to-earth. One neighbor, a local radio host named Mark Madden, lived with his wheelchair-bound mother, who required assistance to get up and down the stairs of Madden's home. Madden fell asleep one day after his mother had gone out to lunch with friends. He awoke to find her in the kitchen, drinking coffee and chatting with Ben Roethlisberger, who had helped her into the house. Madden later recalled:

"It remains one of my fondest memories of her time here. It was something to see."

Thrust Into the Spotlight

As the 2004 football season approached, the Steelers believed they had the luxury of bringing Ben Roethlisberger along gradually. The team had a reliable quarterback in veteran Tommy Maddox, who had started every game for Pittsburgh in 2003. But in week 2 of the 2004 season, in the third quarter of a game against the Baltimore Ravens, Maddox took a hit and came up holding his right elbow. Ben trotted onto the field believing he would take a couple snaps until the veteran shook off the pain. Maddox never returned, however, and Ben had to finish the game for the Steelers.

The rookie had a rough time in his first NFL action. Though he did throw two touchdown passes, he was also picked off twice, and the Ravens returned one of those interceptions for a TD. The Steelers ended up on the short end of a 30–13 score.

The day after the loss, the Steelers received more bad news: Maddox had sustained ligament damage and would be out of the lineup for at least six weeks. Although the season was young and Pittsburgh had won its first game, the Steelers could easily fall out of playoff contention while their starting quarterback was sidelined. So much would depend on how Ben Roethlisberger handled the pressure of filling in at QB. Some of his teammates were openly dismayed at the turn of events, believing Ben wasn't ready. When a reporter asked whether it would be exciting to protect the rookie, **All-Pro** offensive guard Alan Faneca responded incredulously:

Steelers quarterback Tommy Maddox talks with Ben on the sidelines during a 2004 preseason game. Before Ben faced NFL defenses, the Steelers planned to have him observe and learn from the veteran Maddox, who had thrown 38 touchdown passes as Pittsburgh's starting quarterback during the 2002 and 2003 seasons. However, the plan changed when Maddox was injured in the second game of 2004.

❝Exciting? No, it's not exciting. Do you want to go work with some little young kid who's just out of college?❞

Steel City Sensation

The "little young kid" silenced some skeptics on September 26, when he led the Steelers to a 13–3 win against the Miami Dolphins. He won over a few more people the following week, when Pittsburgh topped the Cincinnati Bengals, 28–17. After Ben had engineered a 34–23 win in the Steelers' next game, against the Cleveland Browns,

Alan Faneca declared himself a fan of the man from Findlay. The offensive guard said:

> **"He's making plays and overcoming adversity when he makes a mistake. You can't do anything but take your hat off to him."**

Ben clearly had much to learn, and the Steelers had simplified their offense significantly to help him. Still, he was playing with poise, generally avoiding mistakes, and putting his team in a position to win games.

The rookie faced three tough tests—and passed them all—in Pittsburgh's next three games. He dissected the Dallas Cowboys' defense in week 6, completing 21 of 25 passes for 193 yards and two touchdowns. After a bye week, Ben turned in a nearly identical performance—completing 18 of 24 passes for 196 yards and two TDs—to help his team best the previously unbeaten New England Patriots. In week 9, the Steelers hosted another unbeaten team, the 7–0 Philadelphia Eagles. Philadelphia's renowned blitzing defense couldn't unnerve Big Ben, who again tossed a pair of touchdown passes and led his team to another victory.

By this time, players and coaches around the NFL had taken notice of the rookie QB who was playing like a seasoned veteran. Ken Whisenhunt, Pittsburgh's offensive coordinator, observed:

> **"The thing that surprises me as a rookie in general is, No. 1, his composure under pressure. He also has good field vision, especially when he's on the move. And the third thing is he's smart with the ball. He doesn't make bad decisions."**

Ben had started and won six games in a row. Gone was any thought head coach Bill Cowher had of putting Tommy Maddox back in the lineup when the veteran's elbow was healed.

Pittsburgh fans might have run Cowher out of town for even suggesting that Maddox be restored to the starting role. The Steel

This poster, hung by Steelers fans at the AFC championship game in January 2005, shows the love and admiration the team's young quarterback inspired. Unfortunately, Ben's rookie run of success ended that day with a tough loss to New England. Two weeks later, the Patriots would go on to win Super Bowl XXXIX.

City was in the midst of an uncontrollable outbreak of Big Ben mania. Wherever the quarterback went in public, throngs of well-wishers followed. Stores couldn't keep his #7 Steelers jersey in stock. An area restaurant created—and diners eagerly consumed—a new sandwich, the Roethlis-burger.

The excitement only built as Ben led the Steelers to eight more wins in a row. Pittsburgh finished the regular season with a 15–1 record, best in the NFL, and beat the New York Jets in the divisional playoffs.

The thrill-ride finally ended in the AFC's conference championship game. The New England Patriots intercepted Ben three times and prevailed by a score of 41–37. New England went on to win Super Bowl XXXIX.

Rough Going

In 2004, Big Ben's big arm and steady play had helped bring Pittsburgh to within a game of the Super Bowl. Among the Steelers' faithful, expectations for a championship in 2005 were sky-high.

The season began well, with Pittsburgh winning three of its first four games. But Ben hurt his knee in the Steelers' October 10 win over San Diego. He missed the next game, which Pittsburgh lost, but came back to lead the Steelers to victories in weeks 7 and 8. More knee troubles forced Ben to undergo **arthroscopic surgery**, and he sat out weeks 9, 10, and 11.

Ben returned to the lineup for the Steelers' *Monday Night Football* matchup against the Indianapolis Colts. He seemed rusty after the layoff, throwing for just 133 yards and getting intercepted twice as the Colts prevailed, 26–7. He also hurt the thumb of his right hand, suffering a possible hairline fracture.

Ben had a splint on the thumb for the Steelers' next game, against the Cincinnati Bengals. Though he passed for 386 yards and three touchdowns, he also threw three interceptions. Pittsburgh lost the game, 38–31. Ben was unwilling to use the injured thumb as an excuse for the picks, telling reporters:

"We've got a lot of guys dinged up, and we've got to play through pain. Myself included."

The loss to Cincinnati dropped Pittsburgh's record to 7–5. The team's chances of securing a playoff berth appeared slim.

But then the Steelers caught fire, winning four straight games to finish the regular season with an 11–5 record. They earned a **wild card** slot as the sixth and final **seed** in the AFC.

Making History

Making the playoffs was, of course, a necessary step, but the Steelers knew they faced long odds in order to win the big prize. No sixth seed had ever gone on to the Super Bowl. To become the first team to do so, Pittsburgh would have to win three playoff games on the road.

Ben pitches the ball to wide receiver Antwaan Randle El in the Steelers' 41-0 win over Cleveland, December 24, 2005. This was the third of four straight wins for Pittsburgh, enabling the team to grab the AFC's last playoff spot.

In his second shot at an AFC Championship, Ben had an outstanding game. The Steelers' 34–17 victory over Denver on January 22, 2006, earned the team a spot in Super Bowl XL.

The Steelers took the first step in the wild card game, turning the tables on the Cincinnati Bengals with a 31–17 victory. Ben Roethlisberger posted a solid performance, completing 14 of 19 passes for 208 yards, with three touchdowns and no interceptions.

The following week, in the divisional playoff round, Pittsburgh shocked the Indianapolis Colts. The Steelers' 21–18 win was preserved by Ben's heady play in making "the Tackle."

Next up were the Denver Broncos, who had not lost a game all season in their home stadium, Invesco Field at Mile High. Ben Roethlisberger and the Pittsburgh Steelers would change that in the AFC championship game. Big Ben connected on 21 of 29 passes for 275 yards, threw two touchdown passes, and ran for another score. He also took care of the ball, not getting intercepted or fumbling in the game. The Steelers' 34–17 win in Denver earned them a trip to Super Bowl XL.

Throughout the playoffs, Big Ben had been a model of efficiency. He'd completed 68 percent of his passes and thrown seven touchdown passes while getting picked off just once. In the week before the Super Bowl, wide receiver Hines Ward noted of his quarterback:

CROSS-CURRENTS

The Super Bowl is pro football's biggest stage. For some information on the game's history, see page 51.

Ben dives into the end zone for a one-yard touchdown in the second quarter of Super Bowl XL, February 5, 2006. The score gave the Steelers a 7–3 lead. Pittsburgh would not trail again, defeating the Seahawks by a final score of 21-10.

"He is a second-year guy, but he's the reason why we are here today. We'll go as far as Ben takes us."

Super Bowl XL, played at Detroit's Ford Field on February 5, 2006, figured to be a classic matchup of offense versus defense. The NFC champion Seattle Seahawks were the highest-scoring team in the NFL. Pittsburgh boasted the league's third-ranked defense.

In the end, defense prevailed. Pittsburgh surrendered just 10 points while scoring three touchdowns, the first coming on a one-yard Ben Roethlisberger run in the second quarter. Ben didn't have his best game. He completed just 9 of 21 passes for 123 yards, and he was intercepted twice. But with its 21–10 victory, Pittsburgh had won its fifth Super Bowl, tying the Dallas Cowboys and San Francisco 49ers for the all-time franchise record. And Ben Roethlisberger, at the tender age of 23, had become the youngest starting quarterback ever to lead his team to a Super Bowl victory.

HARD KNOCKS

Ben Roethlisberger seemed to be living a charmed life. He was the toast of Pittsburgh, having brought the football-crazed town its first Super Bowl in more than 25 years. After only two seasons in the NFL, Big Ben was being compared with a Steelers legend, quarterback Terry Bradshaw. Bradshaw's Steelers had won four Super Bowls in six years. Many Pittsburgh fans thought Ben could anchor another dynasty.

Not Invincible

Around 11:30 A.M. on June 12, 2006, Ben was riding his motorcycle near downtown Pittsburgh. He was on his way to the Steelers' training facility to work out. As he approached an intersection, a car going in the opposite direction attempted to make a left-hand turn, and the two vehicles collided. Ben was thrown from his motorcycle. He flew into the car's windshield and landed facedown on the pavement. Ben was not wearing a helmet, and at least one bystander initially thought he was dead.

A paramedic who arrived at the scene closed off a slit blood vessel, preventing Ben from bleeding to death. He was rushed to Mercy Hospital, where he underwent seven hours of surgery to repair multiple fractures to the face, including a broken jaw and a broken nose. He emerged from the surgery in serious but stable condition. Fortunately, the accident hadn't caused severe brain or spinal damage.

The speed with which Ben recovered amazed his doctors. Just a month after the accident, Ben told an interviewer on *Good Morning America* that he would be ready when the Steelers' training camp opened in late July. He also said the accident had taught him a lesson about not taking things for granted:

"I'm coming off of two pretty good seasons in the NFL, winning a Super Bowl and, you know, 24 years old and maybe I felt a little invincible. And this was God's way of saying, 'Hey, I can take it away from you at any time, so you better back off a little bit.'"

CROSS-CURRENTS

Terry Bradshaw led the Pittsburgh Steelers to four Super Bowl titles between 1975 and 1980. Read more about the Hall of Fame quarterback on page 52.

As promised, Ben was ready for the first practice of the Steelers' 2006 training camp in Latrobe, Pennsylvania. Thousands of fans turned out to cheer him on, and teammates and coaches expressed their astonishment at how good Ben looked. Outwardly, he didn't show any effects from the accident.

Big Ben went on to have a fine preseason, and as the 2006 regular season approached, the Steelers set their sights on another championship run. Unfortunately, Ben's travails weren't quite finished. Five days before Pittsburgh's season opener, Ben fell ill at practice.

Pittsburgh police officers look at the badly damaged motorcycle Ben was riding when he was involved in an accident in June 2006. Ben suffered a broken jaw and nose, among other injuries, but he was lucky to survive the crash.

He underwent emergency surgery for appendicitis, sidelining him for the first game.

A Disappointing Season

With backup quarterback Charlie Batch taking the snaps, the Steelers won their opener, a home game against the Miami Dolphins. Ben returned to the lineup in week 2. But he was ineffective, throwing two interceptions as Pittsburgh was blanked by the Jacksonville Jaguars, 9–0. That loss began a three-game skid, during which Ben struggled mightily. He suffered five more interceptions while failing to throw a single touchdown pass.

Ben and the Steelers halted the losing streak in week 6, with a 45–7 pasting of the Kansas City Chiefs. Ben completed 16 of 19 passes for 238 yards, with two TDs and no interceptions. The impressive performance gave Pittsburgh fans hope that the Steelers were back on track.

They weren't. The team dropped three straight games to fall to 2–6 at the halfway point of the season.

Everyone in Pittsburgh—from sportswriters to radio hosts to ordinary fans—seemed ready to offer an opinion as to why the Steelers were struggling. Many people placed the lion's share of blame on Big Ben. Steelers legend Terry Bradshaw, a football analyst for Fox Sports, didn't think that was entirely fair. "You can't put it all on his shoulders," Bradshaw said.

"It's everybody. It's everything—the entire team, the coaching staff. But [Ben] is finding out the other side of being a quarterback—people asking questions, people pointing fingers."

Asked whether he thought Ben might be hampered by injuries, Bradshaw responded:

"Ben is the only person who can say if he's healthy. As far as I'm concerned, it's important to have a quarterback who wants to play, to be on the field, even if he's hurt. It tells your offensive linemen and everybody else on the football team that you're a tough [dude] and that you're tough enough to play through it."

Bradshaw's colleague at Fox, former All-Pro lineman Howie Long, observed that the young quarterback had been through an awful lot in the previous months. "But," Long said, "I like the way Ben has handled himself. . . . I think he's going to come out on [the] other side of this thing."

The Pittsburgh Steelers, at least, came out on the other side of their funk, winning six of their final eight games in 2006. Still, the team's 8–8 record wasn't enough to secure a spot in the postseason. The defending Super Bowl champs would watch the 2006 playoffs from home.

Ben Roethlisberger had staggered through the worst season of his young career. He threw for 18 touchdowns but was intercepted 23 times—more picks than he'd suffered in 2004 and 2005 combined. In each of his first two seasons, Ben's passer rating had topped 98. In 2006, it dropped to 75.4.

Many of Ben's fans wondered whether his motorcycle accident had, in fact, taken a greater toll than anyone had suspected. Critics suggested that he simply wasn't that good a quarterback—that the Steelers' 2004 and 2005 successes had more to do with the greatness of the team than the greatness of its quarterback. Some even questioned Big Ben's work ethic. He bristled at the suggestion that he'd grown complacent, saying:

❝Other than my family, there's nothing I care more about than what I do. I want to be the best that's ever played this game, and I know I'm far from it because of the way I've been playing.❞

Ben went into the 2007 season determined to prove his critics wrong.

Big Ben Rebounds

The Steelers went into the 2007 season with a new head coach. In January, Bill Cowher had resigned after 15 years leading the Steelers. Steelers management quickly hired a replacement: 34-year-old Mike Tomlin, who had been the Minnesota Vikings' defensive coordinator in 2006.

Tomlin and his star quarterback hit it off right away. In March, the new head coach said:

❝Ben has been a breath of fresh air. I love his attitude right now. He's focused. He's committed.❞

That focus and commitment would pay dividends. Shaking off the doldrums of 2006, Big Ben turned in an outstanding 2007 season. He notched 32 touchdown passes against just 11 interceptions. His passer rating of 100.5 was second best in the NFL, behind only Tom Brady of the New England Patriots. Ben's outstanding play earned him his first selection to the **Pro Bowl**. Most important, however, Ben led the Steelers back to their winning ways. With a 10–6 regular-season record, Pittsburgh won the AFC North Division and returned to the playoffs.

On January 5, 2008, the Steelers hosted the 11–5 Jacksonville Jaguars, one of the AFC's wild card teams, in the first

CROSS-CURRENTS

The Pro Bowl pits a team of NFC all-stars against a team of AFC all-stars. For information about the history and rules of this game, see pages 53 and 54.

Ben talks on the sideline with new Steelers head coach Mike Tomlin early in the 2007 season. Tomlin was just 34 years old—younger than some NFL players—when he was hired as Pittsburgh's head coach.

round of the playoffs. To the dismay of the hometown crowd at Heinz Field, Pittsburgh came out flat. Jacksonville took advantage of three Ben Roethlisberger interceptions, one of which was returned for a touchdown, to carry a 21–7 lead into the locker room at halftime. The Jags added another TD in the third quarter while holding Pittsburgh to a field goal. Leading 28–10, Jacksonville appeared firmly in control of the game.

But then Big Ben got going. In the fourth quarter, operating mainly out of the **shotgun** formation, Ben led the Steelers' offense to three touchdowns on three consecutive possessions. He capped the first two drives with touchdown passes, one to wide receiver Santonio Holmes and the other to tight end Heath Miller. On the third drive, with the Steelers at the Jacksonville

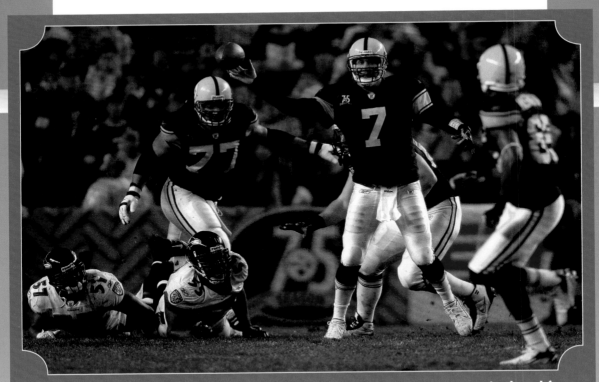

Ben had one of his best games of 2007 against the Baltimore Ravens, Pittsburgh's biggest rival in the AFC North. On November 5, he threw five touchdown passes against Baltimore's tough defense—including this one to Nate Washington (#85, at right). The Steelers romped to an easy victory, 38–7.

one-yard line, Ben handed off to running back Najeh Davenport. Davenport plunged into the end zone, giving the Steelers a 29–28 edge with 6:21 left on the game clock.

But the Jags would spoil the electrifying comeback with a late field goal. The Steelers got the ball back at their own 28-yard line with 47 seconds left. On first down, Ben was sacked. He fumbled, ending Pittsburgh's hopes for a miracle finish.

After the game, the Steelers were quick to rally around their quarterback despite his four turnovers. Tackle Willie Colon told reporters:

"Ben is our leader, he's always going to be our leader. I'll ride or die with him any day. He's tremendous and I love him to death and he led us back."

For the Steelers and their fans, the question was, could Big Ben lead the team back to the top?

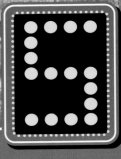

GETTING BACK TO THE TOP

Entering the 2008 season, Ben Roethlisberger had started 62 games for the Steelers. Pittsburgh had won 44 of those games, or 71 percent. Big Ben had a Super Bowl ring to go with that outstanding record of winning. He'd also been recognized as one of the top quarterbacks in the AFC, garnering Pro Bowl honors in 2007.

But, at 26 years old and with four years of NFL experience under his belt, Ben believed he was only beginning to master the quarterback position. In March, the Steelers acknowledged Ben's importance to the team by giving him an eight-year contract extension worth $102 million. That made him the highest-paid player in the NFL for 2008, and the highest-paid player in the history of the Steelers franchise. Ben felt that he had much to prove.

CROSS-CURRENTS

Like other pro athletes, NFL stars make a lot of money. See page 55 for details on contracts and salaries, as well as a list of the highest-paid players.

On a Mission

Ben and the Steelers began the 2008 campaign in fine fashion. They won four of their first five games before their bye week.

After the rest, Pittsburgh alternated wins with losses for a month. The Steelers beat the Cincinnati Bengals in week 6, then fell to the New York Giants, the defending Super Bowl champs, in week 7. They went to Washington and manhandled the Redskins, 23–6, in week 8, only to drop a 24–20 decision at home to the Indianapolis Colts.

Pittsburgh's record stood at 6–3 headed into a week 11 matchup with the San Diego Chargers. That game, played at Heinz Field on November 16, was a nail-biter. But behind Ben Roethlisberger's strong performance—he completed 31 of 41 passes for 308 yards—the Steelers eked out an 11–10 win.

The victory over San Diego marked the beginning of a five-game winning streak. Pittsburgh would finish the 2008 regular season with a 12–4 record, capturing the AFC North crown and gaining a bye in the first round of the playoffs.

Statistically, it hadn't been Ben's best season. He threw just 17 touchdown passes and was picked off 15 times. His passer rating was an unspectacular 80.1. But, as his teammates noted, Ben found ways to win games—and in football that is what counts the most.

The Road to Tampa

On January 11, 2009, Pittsburgh played host to the San Diego Chargers in the divisional playoff round. Steelers fans had some concerns about their quarterback, as Ben had sustained a concussion in the final game of the regular season, a 31–0 blowout of the Cleveland Browns. Ben, however, insisted that he was fine.

The Chargers drew first blood, requiring just two minutes to mount a four-play, 75-yard touchdown drive on the opening possession. Later in the first quarter, Pittsburgh tied the score when Santonio Holmes returned a punt 67 yards for a touchdown.

As Ben and coach Mike Tomlin look on, Pittsburgh Steelers chairman Dan Rooney announces that the team has signed the quarterback to an eight-year contract extension, March 3, 2008. The deal made Ben one of the NFL's highest-paid players.

Defense dominated for most of the second quarter. San Diego got a field goal right after the two-minute warning to go up by a score of 10–7.

The lead wouldn't last long. After the ensuing kickoff, Pittsburgh took over at its own 34-yard line, and Ben Roethlisberger marched his team down the field. Operating from the shotgun, Ben completed three passes, including a 41-yard strike to Hines Ward that took the ball to the Chargers' 3-yard line. From there, Willie Parker ran the ball in, and Pittsburgh held a 14–10 halftime advantage.

At the beginning of the third quarter, Big Ben led the Steelers' offense on a 13-play, 77-yard scoring drive. He completed the drive with an 8-yard touchdown toss to Heath Miller. Pittsburgh now led by a score of 21–10, and San Diego never narrowed that 11-point margin. The final score was 35–24.

Pittsburgh's victory set up a January 18 showdown with the Baltimore Ravens in the AFC championship game. Like the Steelers, Baltimore featured a bruising, relentless defense. The Ravens had given up the third-fewest number of points in the NFL during the 2008 season, whereas the Steelers were first in that category. Analysts expected an old-fashioned, smash-mouth football game in the conference championship. Conditions at Heinz Field only added to that expectation. At kickoff time, 6:30 P.M., the temperature was a frigid 26°F, with a wind chill of 15°F and snow in the forecast.

As anticipated, the game unfolded as a punishing defensive battle. The Steelers managed the only scoring in the first quarter, on two Jeff Reed field goals.

One of Ben's best games of 2008 came on October 5 against Jacksonville. Despite a sore shoulder, he shredded the Jaguars' defense for 309 yards and three touchdowns. The final score came on an eight-yard pass to Hines Ward with 1:53 remaining. It capped an 11-play, 80-yard drive that gave Pittsburgh a 26–21 come-from-behind victory.

At the start of the second quarter, the Steelers' offense faced third-and-nine at their own 35-yard line. Ben Roethlisberger dropped back to pass, and the Ravens brought a blitz. The pocket collapsed, but Ben managed to shed one would-be tackler, scrambled to his left, then danced to his right as two Ravens closed in. He spotted wide receiver Santonio Holmes at midfield and threw across his body. Holmes pulled the ball down and took off, dodging tacklers all the way to the end zone. The 65-yard touchdown put the Steelers up by a score of 13–0. They held on to win, 23–14.

Ben had turned in a solid, workmanlike performance, completing 16 of 33 passes for 255 yards, with one touchdown and no interceptions. But it was his improvised touchdown to Santonio Holmes that Ravens defensive end Trevor Pryce focused on after the game. Pryce offered some advice to the NFC champion Arizona Cardinals:

Ben drops back to pass during the AFC championship game against the Baltimore Ravens, January 18, 2009. His 65-yard touchdown pass early in the second quarter gave Pittsburgh a 13-point lead. The Steelers would go on to defeat the Ravens, 23–14, and return to the Super Bowl for the second time in four years.

"Don't rush Ben Roethlisberger. After that, he's a playground football player. That's what he is, and he's a damn good one."

Super Bowl XLIII

On February 1, 2009, the Pittsburgh Steelers and the Arizona Cardinals faced off at Raymond James Stadium in Tampa, Florida. The game would turn out to be one of the most exciting Super Bowls ever.

Pittsburgh received the opening kickoff, and the Steelers' offense started from their own 28-yard line. On the second play from scrimmage, Ben Roethlisberger connected with Hines Ward for a 38-yard gain that took the ball to Arizona's 32. After two running plays, Big Ben found Heath Miller on a 21-yard pass that set up a first-and-goal from the one. Arizona's defense held firm on first and second downs. On third down, Ben rolled right and dove toward the end zone as he was met by a trio of Cardinals defenders. The officials signaled a touchdown, but Arizona challenged the call, and upon further review it was decided that Ben's knee had touched the ground before the ball broke the plane of the goal line. Facing fourth-and-goal from the one, Steelers head coach Mike Tomlin opted for a field goal, giving Pittsburgh a 3–0 lead.

The Steelers' defense then went to work, shutting down Arizona's offense and forcing a punt. On Pittsburgh's next possession, Big Ben engineered a 69-yard touchdown drive that put the Steelers up by a score of 10–0 early in the second quarter.

Just when it seemed the game might get out of hand, Cardinals quarterback Kurt Warner brought his team back with a touchdown drive on Arizona's next possession. Then, late in the second quarter, Ben Roethlisberger suffered an interception on a tipped pass. The Cardinals' offense took over at the Pittsburgh 34-yard line and drove the ball all the way down to the one. There, facing a first-and-goal with 18 seconds left in the half, Warner dropped back to throw. His pass was intercepted at the goal line by Steelers linebacker James Harrison, who returned the ball 100 yards for a touchdown with no time left on the clock. Harrison's return, the longest play in Super Bowl history, gave Pittsburgh a 17–7 halftime lead.

In the third quarter, Pittsburgh extended its lead to 20–7 with a field goal. The Steelers appeared to be cruising.

But then the Cardinals came roaring back. Midway through the fourth quarter, Arizona got a touchdown on a one-yard toss from Warner to wide receiver Larry Fitzgerald. Then, with about three minutes left in the quarter, Pittsburgh was flagged for a holding penalty in its own end zone, resulting in a safety and two points for the Cardinals. After the free kick, Warner and the Arizona offense took over at their own 34-yard line. On second-and-10, Warner hit Fitzgerald over the middle, and the speedy receiver took the ball 64 yards for a touchdown. The stunning turn of events left the Cardinals holding a 23–20 lead with just 2:37 left in the game.

After the ensuing kickoff, Ben led the Steelers' offense onto the field. The ball was at the Pittsburgh 22-yard line, but a holding penalty took Pittsburgh back to the 12. On first-and-20, Ben scrambled away

An exciting late-game touchdown drive gave Ben the opportunity to hoist the Lombardi Trophy for the second time in his career. Ben performed much better in Super Bowl XLIII than he had in Super Bowl XL. He completed 21 of 30 passes for 256 yards and threw the game-winning touchdown pass. This enabled the Steelers to earn a hard-fought 27–23 victory over the Arizona Cardinals.

from a furious Cardinals rush and found Santonio Holmes for a 14-yard gain. After an incomplete pass on second down, Ben—again under intense pressure—hooked up with Holmes for a 13-yard pass play. An 11-yard completion to wide receiver Nate Washington and a Big Ben scramble for 4 yards took the ball past midfield. Then Ben hit Holmes for 40 yards, taking the ball all the way to the Cardinals' 6-yard line. After an incomplete pass on first down, Ben feathered a pass to Holmes—who was triple-covered—at the back right corner of the end zone. Holmes hauled in the perfectly thrown ball and managed to get both feet inbounds for the TD. Just 35 seconds remained on the clock.

Big Ben had engineered one of the most thrilling late-game drives in Super Bowl history, thereby solidifying his claim as a clutch quarterback. The Steelers held on to win, 27–23. It was the franchise's record-setting sixth Super Bowl title.

Simply a Winner

Ben Roethlisberger may never be as flashy as a Peyton Manning or as smooth as a Tom Brady. But he is, without a doubt, every bit as much a winner. He has two Super Bowl rings to prove it.

And, after the 2009 campaign—another outstanding individual year for Big Ben, though the Steelers finished 9–7 and out of the playoffs—the six-year player could point to some career numbers that ought to silence critics. He'd compiled a postseason winning percentage of .800. He'd completed 63.3 percent of his career pass attempts, slightly higher than San Francisco 49ers legend Joe Montana (63.2 percent). His passer rating of 91.7 was higher than that of Dan Marino, Jim Kelly, Roger Staubach, Troy Aikman, John Elway, and many other quarterbacks enshrined in the Pro Football Hall of Fame in Canton, Ohio.

Barring a serious injury, Canton may also beckon Big Ben one day.

History of the Pittsburgh Steelers

In 1933, Art Rooney of Pittsburgh had a great day at the racetrack. He won $2,500 betting on horses. Rooney used his winnings to establish a team in the National Football League. The team was named the Pirates after Pittsburgh's long-established baseball team.

It took Rooney's team nearly 10 years to produce a winning record. By then, the team had become the Steelers, a name reflecting Pittsburgh's central place in the nation's steel industry. The Steelers finally made the playoffs in 1947, but they lost in the first round.

Getting Better

For the next 20 years the Steelers were mediocre. They hit rock bottom in 1968 and 1969, winning a total of just three games. The seeds of future greatness, however, were being sown. Chuck Noll became coach before the 1969 season, and he chose defensive tackle "Mean" Joe Greene in the draft that year. The following year he took quarterback Terry Bradshaw. The

Since 2001, the Steelers have played their home games in Heinz Field, which is located along the Ohio River in Pittsburgh. The stadium seats more than 65,000 fans.

two players became the team's offensive and defensive leaders during the 1970s.

In 1972, the Steelers won their first-ever division title. Their first-round playoff game against Oakland featured one of the most famous plays in NFL history, the "Immaculate Reception." With 22 seconds left, Pittsburgh trailed, 7–6. On fourth down, Bradshaw scrambled, then hurled a pass far downfield. An Oakland defensive back broke up the play, and the ball flew into the air. Steelers rookie running back Franco Harris, trailing the play, alertly snatched the ball just before it hit the turf. He ran downfield to score the winning touchdown.

Although the Steelers lost in the next week's AFC championship game that year, Pittsburgh's first playoff win set the stage for the team's glory years. Anchored by the "Steel Curtain" defense, Pittsburgh won the Super Bowl in 1975, 1976, 1979, and 1980. They became the first NFL team to win four Super Bowls.

The Cowher Era

For more than a decade after that fourth Super Bowl victory, however, the Steelers didn't do well. As stars like Bradshaw, Greene, wide receivers Lynn Swann and John Stallworth, and linebackers Jack Lambert and Jack Ham retired, the Steelers struggled to make the playoffs.

The team's fortunes improved when Bill Cowher replaced Noll in 1992, and the team made the playoffs six years in a row. The Steelers advanced to the Super Bowl in 1996 but lost to Dallas, 27–17. Their fifth Super Bowl win came a decade later. The 21–10 victory over the Seattle Seahawks tied Pittsburgh with San Francisco and Dallas for the most Super Bowl triumphs.

A New Coach

Cowher retired after the 2006 season and was replaced by Mike Tomlin—just the third Steelers head coach in nearly 40 years. As is evident from the long tenure of Pittsburgh's coaches, the Rooney family—which still owns the team—values stability. Many football insiders say this has been a key ingredient in the franchise's success.

At the time he took the Pittsburgh job, Mike Tomlin was 34 years old, which is quite young for an NFL head coach. The previous season, he had been defensive coordinator for the Minnesota Vikings. Before that, Tomlin did a five-year stint as defensive backs coach for the Tampa Bay Buccaneers.

Pittsburgh's decision to hire Tomlin paid dividends quickly. In 2008, his second season at the helm of the Steelers, Tomlin coached the team to an NFC North Division title and an AFC championship. On February 1, 2009, he became the youngest head coach to win the Super Bowl, as his Steelers defeated the Arizona Cardinals, 27–23, in Super Bowl XLIII. (Go back to page 6.) ◄◄

The NFL Draft

Each year the NFL conducts what is officially termed a player selection meeting, commonly called the draft. This is the process by which the NFL brings new players from the ranks of college football into the league.

The draft is organized into a series of seven rounds. In each round, each of the 32 NFL teams gets to pick a player. The order in which teams pick is determined by their success the previous year. The team with the worst record gets the first choice. The team with the second-worst record gets the second choice, and so on. The Super Bowl winner gets the last pick of the round. The draft is organized this way to try to balance the talent levels among the teams. Teams can change the order of their pick, however, if they trade a player. The Super Bowl winner, for example, could trade a star player for a higher pick.

The draft takes place near the end of April, and it is a huge media event. The top players usually attend and dress well for the event. Fans often boo or cheer a particular pick.

For NFL coaches and team executives, however, the hype is beside the point. Their focus is on getting the players who will most be able to help their team win. A good draft can greatly improve a team's performance—and in some cases, the improvement is immediate. On the other hand, several bad picks can hamper a club's chances for years to come.

Diamonds in the Rough

In the early years of the NFL, teams often did not know much about the players they drafted. They depended on word of mouth or phone calls to sportswriters or college coaches. That is no longer the case. Scouting has become a science. Enormous files are maintained on prospects. Would-be draftees are weighed, measured, timed, and even given intelligence and psychological tests.

Most of the time, this homework pays off. A recent study of All-Pro players over the last five years showed that half were drafted in the first round.

Sometimes, however, players have slipped through the cracks. In the 2002 draft, for example, 90 players were selected before the Eagles finally chose Brian Westbrook in the third round. And occasionally, a player is completely overlooked on draft day, only to go on to have a Hall of Fame NFL career. Undrafted Hall of Famers include quarterback Warren Moon, and defensive backs Willie Brown and Dick "Night Train" Lane. Current New England Patriots star wide receiver Wes Welker was not chosen on draft day in 2004. (Go back to page 19.) ◀◀

Quarterback Controversy

The 2004 college football draft class contained several highly touted quarterbacks. They included Eli Manning of the University of Mississippi, a Heisman Trophy finalist; North Carolina State's Philip Rivers; and, after his stellar junior season at Miami, Ben Roethlisberger. Manning—the son of former NFL quarterback Archie Manning and the brother of Indianapolis Colts QB Peyton Manning, an All-Pro— was generally regarded as the best of the bunch. In fact, many football experts considered him the 2004 draft's top prospect at any position.

In the lead-up to the draft, however, Manning ignited a firestorm of controversy when his agent informed the San Diego Chargers—the team with the first overall pick—that they should not draft him. This was not simply friendly advice. There was an implied threat that, if Chargers management did go ahead and draft him, Manning would refuse to play for the team. He could sit out a year and reenter the draft in 2005, in which case San Diego would get nothing at all for the number-one pick.

Quarterback Eli Manning (#10) made it clear before the 2004 NFL draft that he did not want to play in San Diego. He has been the Giants' starting quarterback since 2005. In February 2008, Manning led New York to a 17–14 upset victory over the New England Patriots in Super Bowl XLII. He was named the game's Most Valuable Player.

Manning's representatives, including his father, made it known that the young quarterback had no interest in playing for a losing franchise, and San Diego had failed to post a winning season in the previous eight years. The Manning camp suggested that the New York Giants would be "a good fit."

The idea that someone who had never played a single down in the NFL would try to dictate which team could employ his services rubbed many football fans the wrong way. Manning was criticized as an immature, selfish prima donna.

Ben Roethlisberger's attitude couldn't have been more different from that of the Ole Miss star. Asked whether he was concerned about being drafted by a bad team, Ben responded:

❝Are you kidding me? [Playing in the NFL is] every football player's dream. I don't care where I go, I don't care what they ask of me. I can't wait for draft day.❞

On April 24, when draft day arrived, the Chargers did in fact select Eli Manning with the first overall pick. But they had worked out a trade to accommodate his demands while still getting a good return for the number-one pick. San Diego sent Manning to New York for Rivers—whom the Giants had selected fourth—along with three New York draft picks. (Go back to page 21.) ◀◀

Philip Rivers (#17) is shown here in the red jersey during a team practice. Since becoming the Chargers' starting quarterback in 2006, Rivers has led the team to the playoffs every season.

The Super Bowl

Although the first Super Bowl was played in 1967, its roots go back to 1960, when the American Football League (AFL) was formed to compete with the long-established National Football League (NFL). The AFL quickly became a strong rival to the older league.

By the mid-1960s, owners in both leagues were concerned that the competition between them was driving the players' salaries too high. The owners decided to merge the two leagues and form a single league. It would take several years to work out the details of the merger. One of the conditions, however, was that the winner of one league would play the winner of the other in a championship game.

The NFL's Most Famous Ball

At first, Pete Rozelle, the head of the NFL, wanted to call this game "The Big One." Then one day, Kansas City Chiefs owner Lamar Hunt came up with a different name. He was watching his children play with a Super Ball, and that toy gave him the idea of calling the game the "Super Bowl." He doubted this nickname would last very long, but he was wrong. Today, the Super Ball that the Hunt children played with is in the Professional Football Hall of Fame.

In the first Super Bowl in 1967, the Green Bay Packers easily defeated Lamar Hunt's Kansas City Chiefs, 35–10. The game's result was nearly the same the following year, with a 33–14 Packer win over the Oakland Raiders. These two wins seemed to confirm many fans' beliefs that the NFL had a higher quality of play.

The Namath Guarantee

In 1969, nearly everyone expected the third game to follow the same pattern. The NFL's Baltimore Colts were 18-point favorites over the AFL's New York Jets. Jets quarterback Joe Namath, however, guaranteed that his team would win. He backed up his words on the field, and his team emerged with a 16–7 win, one of the greatest upsets in American sports history. When the AFL champion Chiefs defeated the NFL champion Minnesota Vikings 23–7 the following year, doubts about the competitive differences between the leagues disappeared.

By the start of the 1970 season, the merger was complete. The new league was known as the National Football League. Its then-26 teams were divided into two conferences: the American Football Conference (AFC), which consisted of 10 AFL teams plus 3 former NFL teams, and the National Football Conference (NFC), which consisted of the 13 remaining NFL teams. From then on, the Super Bowl would match the two conference winners.

Today, the Super Bowl is the single most-watched television event in the United States. Super Bowl Sunday has almost become a national holiday. (Go back to page 28.) ◀◀

Terry Bradshaw

In the midst of his first season in the NFL, some Pittsburgh fans had already begun comparing Ben Roethlisberger with Terry Bradshaw, an icon of the Steelers franchise. After the 2005 season, when Ben quarterbacked the team to a Super Bowl victory, those comparisons only multiplied. Big Ben understood the huge expectations that went along with the comparisons. "I'm trying to fill some pretty big shoes in Pittsburgh," he said in 2006.

Big shoes indeed. Bradshaw quarterbacked the Steelers to four Super Bowl titles in six years.

Born in 1948 in Shreveport, Louisiana, Terry Bradshaw was a collegiate star at Louisiana Tech. Like Ben Roethlisberger, he was a big QB, standing 6'3" tall and weighing 215 pounds. He also had a very strong arm.

In 1970, the Steelers selected Bradshaw with the first overall pick in the NFL draft. Early on, he struggled, throwing 24 interceptions and just six touchdown passes in his first season. Many critics predicted that he would never succeed in the NFL. They were wrong. After adjusting to the pro game, Bradshaw became one of the most dominant QBs in the league.

In January 1975, he quarterbacked the Steelers to a 16–6 victory over the Minnesota Vikings in Super Bowl IX. It was the team's first Super Bowl. The following year, with Bradshaw calling the plays, the Steelers repeated as NFL champs. They also won Super Bowls XIII and XIV, in 1979 and 1980. Bradshaw was named MVP of both of those games.

Terry Bradshaw retired after the 1982 season. He was inducted into the Pro Football Hall of Fame in 1989. (Go back to page 31.) ◀◀

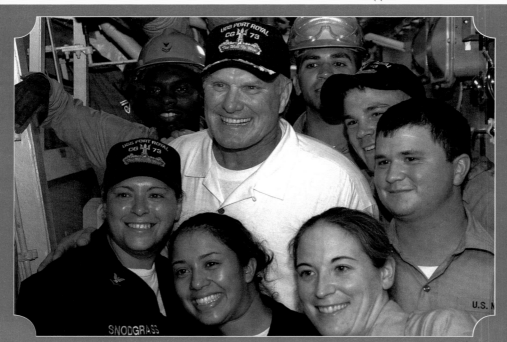

Terry Bradshaw, a member of the Pro Football Hall of Fame, poses with admiring fans during a visit to a U.S. Navy ship.

The Pro Bowl

The NFL is the only major professional sports league that holds its annual all-star game after the regular season ends. Major League Baseball, the National Basketball Association, and the National Hockey League hold their all-star games in the middle of their seasons.

The first NFL-sponsored all-star game was played in early 1939, after the end of the 1938 season. The NFL champions, the New York Giants, beat a collection of all-stars from other NFL teams and two independent teams, 13–10. This version of the game, with the NFL champion playing a group of all-stars, continued for four years until World War II interrupted the NFL's play.

The all-star game resumed after the 1950 season and pitted the all-stars of the NFL's American Conference against the all-stars of the National Conference. After the NFL was realigned into East and West divisions in 1953, the game matched up the best players in the East with the best in the West. That arrangement continued until the NFL formally merged with the American Football League (AFL) in 1970. The game, now called the Pro Bowl, became a matchup between the best players in the AFC and NFC.

Three groups—the fans, players, and coaches—vote on who will play for the NFC and AFC in the Pro Bowl. Each group has one-third of the voting power, to prevent fans of one team or one particular player from dominating the vote. Before 1995, only coaches and players were allowed to vote.

Starting in 1951, the Pro Bowl began giving a Most Valuable Player (MVP) award. From 1957 to 1971, the game presented two awards—one for the most valuable offensive back and one for the most valuable defensive lineman. One year later, two MVP awards were given, one to the best offensive player and the other to the best defensive player. Since 1973, however, only one MVP award has been given.

Some players look forward to the Pro Bowl as an opportunity for a postseason vacation. The game has grown into a weeklong celebration. The week before the game, there are numerous parties, an NFL alumni touch football game, a celebrity golf tournament, and a football skills contest.

From 1980 through 2009, the Pro Bowl was played at Aloha Stadium in Honolulu, Hawaii. In 2010, the game was held in Dolphin Stadium in south Florida. The date of the game was also changed for 2010. The Pro Bowl used to be held a week after the Super Bowl, but in 2010 the game was played on the Sunday before Super Bowl XLIV. This meant that players whose teams had reached the NFL's championship game would not be able to participate in the Pro Bowl. Some other players feel honored to be selected but choose not to play, so they can rest and recover from the long NFL season.
(Go back to page 35.) ◄◄

Pro Bowl Rules

The Pro Bowl has been called the least intense game on the NFL schedule. Still, there is always the chance that a player might get seriously injured during the game, so the Pro Bowl is played under a special set of rules.

Under Pro Bowl rules, the offense isn't allowed to shift before the ball is snapped. The offense also is not allowed to send a receiver in motion, and it has to have a tight end on every play. The offense can't line up more than three receivers on one side.

To protect the quarterback, the defense isn't allowed to blitz. The defense is also required to line up in a 4-3 formation on every play, and it can't use more than four defensive backs to cover receivers. Unlike in regular-season games, the quarterback is free to throw the ball away, without penalty, if all of his receivers are covered.

Place kickers and punters are also protected under Pro Bowl rules. The special teams can't rush a kicker during a field goal attempt, on a punt, or during a point-after-touchdown (PAT) kick. A fan watching the Pro Bowl won't see any blocked kicks.

While you're not likely to see any bone-jarring hits during the Pro Bowl, you will see the best players in the NFL play an entertaining, wide-open, high-scoring, end-of-the-season exhibition game. (Go back to page 35.) ◀◀

The stricter rules in place for Pro Bowl games help to ensure that the NFL's star players won't be injured while playing in the annual all-star exhibition game.

Money and the NFL

In the early days of professional football, players took the field for little more than a "sawbuck" —$10—and a pat on the back. But over the last 30 years, with the arrival of players unions and televised games, salaries have skyrocketed.

In 1994, in an effort to slow the rise in player salaries and to help owners control costs, the NFL put in place a salary cap for its players. This means that no team can spend more than a specified amount of money to pay the salaries of all the players on its roster. At the outset, the cap was set at $34.6 million annually. The cap is adjusted each year based on the amount of money the NFL earns. As of 2008 it stood at $116 million.

To afford their high-performing playmakers, team presidents craft complex contracts, which typically include bonuses, options, and deferred payments that spread costs out over a number of years in order to allow the team to meet a given year's salary cap. For the 2008 season, Ben Roethlisberger was the highest-paid player in the NFL, making $27.7 million in compensation that would count toward the salary cap. That worked out to about $1.45 million per game, including the postseason. The second-highest-paid player for 2008 was defensive end Jared Allen of the Minnesota Vikings, who received about $21.1 million. Wide receiver Larry Fitzgerald of the Arizona Cardinals was third on the 2008 money list, taking in $17.1 million. Rounding out the top five were second-year Oakland Raiders quarterback JaMarcus Russell, whose $16.8 million in compensation seemed way out of balance with his mediocre performance; and running back Michael Turner, whom the Atlanta Falcons signed as a free agent for $16 million.

Of course, the average NFL salary is considerably lower. The minimum salary for an NFL rookie in 2008 was $295,000. Each year of experience in the league guarantees a larger minimum salary.

Still, payroll costs for NFL teams are enormous. About two-thirds of all revenue generated by NFL teams each year goes to the players. In May 2008, NFL commissioner Roger Goodell announced that the league might extend the 16-game season by one game to increase team owners' profits. (Go back to page 39.) ◀◀

1982   Ben Roethlisberger is born in Lima, Ohio, on March 2.

1992   Family moves to Findlay, Ohio.

1996   Enters Findlay High School.

2000   Enters Miami of Ohio as physical education major. Redshirts during his first year.

2001   Becomes Miami's starting quarterback.

2003   Leads Miami to a 13–1 season and a #10 national ranking. Sets numerous school passing records. After the GMAC Bowl, in which he is named MVP, announces that he will skip his senior year to enter NFL draft.

2004   Selected by the Pittsburgh Steelers in the first round of the NFL draft (11th pick overall). Becomes Pittsburgh's starting quarterback in third game of 2004 season, and leads team to 14 straight victories before a loss in the AFC championship.

2005   Knee injuries force him to miss four games during the regular season, but he leads Steelers to an AFC championship.

2006   Becomes youngest quarterback (23 years old) in NFL history to win a Super Bowl, as Pittsburgh beats Seattle, 21–10. Suffers a serious motorcycle accident on June 12. Has an emergency appendectomy five days before the start of the 2006 season. Has worst season statistically, and Pittsburgh misses playoffs.

2007   Has outstanding season, throwing 32 touchdown passes against just 11 interceptions, and leads Pittsburgh to a first-place finish in AFC North Division. Steelers lose to the Jacksonville Jaguars in wild card round of playoffs.

2008   In March, signs eight-year, $102 million contract extension with Pittsburgh. Leads team to a 12–4 record, good for first place in the AFC North. Sustains a concussion in the last game of the regular season.

2009   On February 1, engineers a late-game drive to give the Steelers a come-from-behind, 27–24 win over the Arizona Cardinals in Super Bowl XLIII. Pittsburgh finishes the 2009 season with a 9–7 record and misses the playoffs.

Career Statistics

Year	Team	G	GS	Comp	Att	Pct	Yds	Avg	TD	Int	Rate
2004	Pittsburgh Steelers	14	13	196	295	66.4	2,621	8.9	17	11	98.1
2005	Pittsburgh Steelers	12	12	168	268	62.7	2,385	8.9	17	9	98.6
2006	Pittsburgh Steelers	15	15	280	469	59.7	3,513	7.5	18	23	75.4
2007	Pittsburgh Steelers	15	15	164	404	65.3	3,154	7.8	32	11	104.1
2008	Pittsburgh Steelers	16	16	181	469	59.9	3,301	7.0	17	15	80.1
2009	Pittsburgh Steelers	15	15	337	506	66.6	4,328	8.6	26	12	100.5
Total		87	86	1326	2,411	380.6	19,302	48.7	127	81	91.7

Key:
    G = games
    GS = games started
    Comp = passes completed
    Att = passes attempted
    Pct = completion percentage
    Yds = total passing yards
    Avg = average yards per pass
    TD = touchdown passes
    Int = interceptions
    Rate = passer rating

Awards

College:
        MAC Freshman of the Year (2001)
        Football Writer's Association of America Freshman All-America First Team (2001)
        All-MAC Second Team (2002)
        MAC Most Valuable Player (2003)
        All-MAC First Team (2003)
        All-America Third Team (2003)

NFL:

        Rookie of the Year (2004)
        Pro Bowl (2007)

Books

Giglio, Joe. *Great Teams in Pro Football History* (Great Teams series). Chicago: Raintree, 2006.

Koestler-Grack, Rachel A. *Ben Roethlisberger* (Football Superstars series). New York: Chelsea House, 2008.

Rooney, Dan, as told to Andrew E. Masich and David F. Halaas. *Dan Rooney: My 75 Years with the Pittsburgh Steelers and the NFL*. Cambridge, MA: Da Capo Press, 2007.

Six Times Super: The Official Book of the Super Bowl XLIII Champion Pittsburgh Steelers. Introduction and foreword by Art Rooney II. Foreword by Dan Rooney. Indianapolis: Steeler Digest/Curtis Publishing, 2009.

Stewart, Mark. *The Pittsburgh Steelers* (Team Spirit series). Chicago: Norwood House Press, 2006.

Web Sites

http://www.bigbennews.com/articles.htm
This site provides a compilation of articles about Ben Roethlisberger.

http://www.bigben7.com/foundation.aspx
Ben Roethlisberger's official Web site focuses on his charitable organization, the Ben Roethlisberger Foundation.

http://www.nfl.com/players/benroethlisberger/profile?id=ROE750381
The Ben Roethlisberger page on the NFL's Web site has career stats for the Pittsburgh quarterback, as well as videos of game action.

http://www.steelers.com/
The official Web site of the Pittsburgh Steelers includes the team's roster, schedule, statistics, news, merchandise, and more.

All-Pro—a football player voted best at his position in the entire NFL for a given season; ballots are cast by a panel of national sports-media members.

arthroscopic surgery—a surgical procedure (often performed on joints such as the knee and the shoulder), in which the surgeon uses a small scope with a camera, avoiding the larger incisions that are necessary with traditional surgery.

blitz—in football, a play in which a defensive back or linebacker joins down linemen in rushing the quarterback.

blue-collar—working-class; characteristic of wage laborers rather than salaried professionals.

gridiron—a football field.

Heisman Trophy—an award given each year to the top college football player, as chosen by a group of national sportswriters.

passer rating—a statistic that measures a quarterback's passing efficiency through a formula that includes his completion percentage, passing yardage, touchdowns, and interceptions.

possession—in football, an instance when the offensive team has the ball.

Pro Bowl—the NFL's annual all-star game, usually played in Hawaii the week after the Super Bowl.

recruit—to try to secure the services of a person; in sports, to get a high school athlete to commit to a particular college.

redshirt—an athlete who works out with a team but doesn't compete during his first year at college, in order to preserve four full years of eligibility for competition under NCAA rules.

sack—an instance when the quarterback is tackled behind the line of scrimmage for a loss.

seed—a ranked spot in a tournament or postseason competition.

shotgun—an offensive formation, used in passing situations, in which the quarterback lines up several yards in the backfield rather than directly under the center.

tandem—a group of two people or things used together.

wild card—one of two teams in each of the NFL's conferences that makes the playoffs without winning its division; the first round of the NFL playoffs.

page 11 "very lucky," Joe Starkey, "Big Ben Makes Game-Saving Tackle," *Pittsburgh Tribune-Review*, January 16, 2006. http://www.bigbennews. com/articles/2006/thetackle.html

page 11 "It's one of those . . ." Associated Press, "Thanks to Big Ben, Bettis' Fumble Not Costly," NBC Sports online, January 16, 2006. http:// nbcsports.msnbc.com/id/10869900/

page 11 "Ben saved the year . . ." Associated Press, "Thanks to Big Ben."

page 14 "Even when he was 15 . . ." David Fleming, "For Whom the Ben Tolls," *ESPN The Magazine*, February 2005. http://www.bigbennews.com/ articles/2005/forwhomthebentolls. html

page 18 "I broke every roommate rule . . ." Fleming, "For Whom the Ben Tolls."

page 20 "From what I can tell . . ." Shelly Anderson, "The Real Life," *Pittsburgh Post-Gazette*, May 2, 2004. http://www.bigbennews.com/ articles/2004/thereallife.html

page 21 "It remains one of my fondest . . ." Daniel Malloy and Timothy McNulty, "For Roethlisberger, Complications Grow," *Pittsburgh Post-Gazette*, August 10, 2009. http://www.post-gazette.com/pg/09222/989873-66. stm

page 22 "Exciting? No, it's not . . ." "Rookie Steps in for Injured Maddox," *ESPN. com*, September 27, 2004. http:// sports.espn.go.com/nfl/news/ story?id=1885470

page 23 "He's making plays . . ." Douglas Lederman, "Roethlisberger Stays off His Own Bandwagon," *USA Today*, October 14, 2004.

page 25 "The thing that surprises me . . ." Dennis Dillon, "Roethlisberger Sizzles with Meaty Performance," *Sporting News*, November 1, 2004. http:// www.bigbennews.com/articles/2004/ roethlisbergermeaty.html

page 27 "We've got a lot of guys . . ." Alan Robinson, "Bengals 38, Steelers 31," *Yahoo! Sports*, December 4, 2005. http://sports.yahoo.com/nfl/recap;_ ylt=AkBodjKXNHTlDLtJYpmEoOj. uLYF?gid=20051204023

page 29 "He is a second-year . . ." Sean Jensen, "Big Ben Big Part of Steelers Success," *Monterey Herald*, February 4, 2006. http://www.bigbennews.com/ articles/2006/bigbenbigpart.html

page 31 "I'm coming off . . ." Ben Roethlisberger interview, ABC News *Good Morning America*, July 14, 2006.

page 33 "You can't put it all . . ." Robert Dvorchak, "Bradshaw Can Relate to Pressure on Big Ben," *Pittsburgh Post-Gazette*, November 11, 2006.

page 33 "Ben is the only person . . ." Dvorchak, "Bradshaw Can Relate."

page 33 "But I like the way Ben . . ." Dvorchak, "Bradshaw Can Relate."

page 34 "Other than my family . . ." Scott Brown, "Steelers Big Ben Takes Steps to Regain Top Form," *Pittsburgh Tribune-Review*, March 4, 2007. http://www.bigbennews.com/ articles/2007/steelersbigbentakes.html

page 34 "Ben has been a breath . . ." Scott Brown, Roethlisberger Impressing New Steelers Coach," *Pittsburgh Tribune-Review*, March 28, 2007. http://www. bigbennews.com/articles/2007/ roethlisbergerimpressing.html

page 37 "Ben is our leader . . ." Associated Press, "Jaguars Relinquish 18-point Lead but Stun Steelers at End," *ESPN.com*, January 5, 2008. http://sports.espn.go.com/nfl/recap?gameId=280105023

page 42 "Don't rush Ben Roethlisberger . . ." Associated Press, "Polamalu's INT Return Secures Steelers' Super Bowl Berth," *ESPN.com*, January 18, 2009. http://espn.go.com/nfl/recap?gameId=290118023

page 50 "a good fit," Jim Trotter, "Manning to Bolts: Don't Draft Me," *San Diego Union-Tribune*, April 22, 2004. http://legacy.signonsandiego.com/sports/chargers/20040422-9999-1s22chargers.html

page 50 "Are you kidding me? . . ." Josh Elliot, "Almost Famous," *Sports Illustrated On Campus*, April 15, 2004. http://sportsillustrated.cnn.com/2004/sioncampus/04/14/roethlisberger0415/

page 52 "I'm trying to fill . . ." Jensen, "Big Ben Big Part."

Rudolph T. Heits was born and raised in West Texas. His books include *DeMarcus Ware* and *Jason Witten* in Mason Crest's SUPERSTARS OF PRO FOOTBALL series.

PICTURE CREDITS